Suntzu's Art of War In Thirteen Acts

By Peter Hainzl

Introduction:

Welcome to The Art of War

So, my dear reader, after hearing about an ancient Zhou Dynasty general named Suntzu and his book The Art of War, you have managed to score yourself a copy.

You are flicking through the pages and now find yourself drowning in verbose words that make no sense, no matter how sagely they appear.

It's not like you are going off to war, real war, but everybody is telling you that The Art of War is supposed to help you in whatever game you got going.

But that's not happening.

But don't worry. Literally, you are not alone. Most people who buy the book, read a couple of pages. And after having their eyes fogged over one too many times, put the book down and pretty much never touch it again.

So what's the difference between those who 'get it' and those who don't?

Only one thing really.

And the Art of War, without actually mentioning it, assumes that you have got it.

But you don't.

It's a bit like algebra. You, like most people have been taught that the way to find out what 'x' is, is to use the formula given in the equation. 'X' is found by elimination of the fluff around it.

Suntzu never dealt with people like that. His bosses were the kind of people that told you what 'x' will be regardless of the algebra equation. In their world, if 'x' was five but the answer was three, then five it was. And everything else around it had to change to fit the answer.

The point is, they decided beforehand what the answer or goal would be. And not the other way round as is the case with most people.

The reason why The Art of War makes no sense is because you don't have a goal.

Without a goal, none of the thirteen chapters can align themselves properly to achieve something worthwhile. That's sagely advice for you to get yourself a goal first.

So until then, you're never really gonna 'get it' because until then you don't need general Suntzu's book The Art of War.

Chapter One:

What do the numbers say?

It is said in the Art of War that war is as critical to a country as life and death. And because the winds of fortune are forever changing, an apt leader will study it carefully.

Therefore the first chapter, sometimes called Calculations, deals heavily with the numbers involved, and in its essence asks if the resources are really there to back up the will?

ACT ONE

King: I want to attack my neighbour!

Sage: So you want to attack your neighbour?

King: That's what I said.

Sage: Ok then. Um, Why are we doing this?

King: Because I think... (blah, blah, blah)... and so because I am the king, I have justified my list of reasons as ordained by the will of heaven.

Sage: Right! And supposedly it is a good idea, directly and indirectly the people will suffer, somewhat, regardless of the outcome. What exactly do I tell the people?

King: The people? What have they got to do with anything?

Sage: Well, um, let's just say it doesn't go to plan. Spin-doctors haven't been invented yet.

King: But I really want to go to war!

Sage: My lord, do you know if we even have enough soldiers and provisions to successfully fight and win?

King: Provisions?

Sage: Yes My lord. This so-called heaven mandated goal is a heavily yang orientated ambition. But the people are by nature yin and they will be supplying the men, food, equipment and money needed.

King: I see. Well, in that case, as my appointed Sage, I hereby appoint you to War Minister. Now be a good chap and sort it out for me.

Sage, known henceforth as the War Minister a.k.a. Sima: My lord.

Chapter Two:

How many steps does it take to get to the top of the mountain?

Just as the first chapter assumes that you have a goal that you want to achieve, the second chapter assumes that you have crunched the numbers, found them favourable and have made the decision to go ahead with it.

The key point to chapter two is that you have decided. And with that decision comes the need for a map.

The reason why Suntzu continues with the numbers theme, but in a different way, is that the hidden secret behind maps is that maps have a way of reducing costs in terms of time and distance travelled.

ACT TWO

Sima: The king has decided to go to war.

General: Wow there! We can't just go and fight. We need to prepare.

King: What seems to be the problem?

Sima: No problem my Lord. The general just has a few 'nagging' concerns.

King: Speak my General.

General: My Lord, if we are going to attack our neighbour, I am going to have to put in a request for a few things. Set some conditions. Make sure that the donkey is in front of the cart. That sort of thing.

King: The donkey in front of the cart? Donkey? Cart? General, I thought the army uses chariots?

Sima: Apologies my lord. That was a poorly timed figure of speech. General, I believe you were placing a request for items needed to win this war of conquest for the king?

General: Well, Sima, since the boss is picking up the tab, let's see... um... Oh here's my list.... First item, one hundred thousand soldiers. No wait. We are fighting our other enemy. Make that two hundred thousand men. Second item...

Chapter Three:

So what's the game plan?

This is the chapter from which we get the often quoted famous saying: No thy enemy, no thyself.

And a lot of the chapter, usually called Strategy, is a series of navel gazing questions a person in the business of war must ask of themselves.

It all boils down to this: Are you good enough to fit the role? Does the man (or woman) fit the clothes?

It's not one size fits all. A good leader must select the right general and the right strategy to achieve the right aim in the right way.

ACT THREE

King: Ok people. Listen up! We've got the men, the horses and all the rest. Now let's go and attack them!

Sima: My Lord?

King: Yes?

Sima: Do you remember what happened to your father?

King: Yes. And so?

Sima: My lord, wouldn't it be more impressive if the outcome this time was different this time? Marching two hundred thousand men over the border is hard work.

King: And your point is?

Sima: My lord, you know, if you could defeat your neighbour without killing anybody that would be really impressive.

King: I see, and how do you propose to do this impressive thing?

Sima: Well, my lord, me and the boys have come up with a strategy!

Chapter Four:

Defend first - Attack later, why?

It is often said that a good defence is a good offence. The people who like to use this saying usually have no grasp of the outcomes of war. Rarely do they realise that for the side starting a war, it more often than not ends in disaster.

Hence, in chapter four, Suntzu bestoles the virtues of having good strategic defence like Switzerland: Good naturally strong defences backed up by a strong army. And more importantly, in the larger scheme of things, a country at peace with itself. Countries at peace with themselves rarely attack other countries and other countries rarely attack them.

Suntzu wasn't a pussy. He just better understood than most, that what his boss really wanted was power, prestige and wealth (against his rivals). And so, a good sage needs to delicately sometimes remind a king of the Mafia saying, "You can't make money with a gun in your hand!"

ACT FOUR

King: So this is a map of the world before me. How is it supposed to help me win? Can't we just go in and smash a few heads and be done with it?

Sima: My lord, it doesn't work that way. Based on current intel', their defensive positions are quite strong here, here and here.

King: I see. And you'd advise me to take this alternative route instead?

Sima: Only as a strongly worded consideration, my lord. But the generals consider this plan more fortuitous to your wishes.

King: I still don't think your strategy will work. The people demand glory on the battlefield.

Sima: But my lord, quote, the people, unquote, will not be doing the fighting. The army will.

King: So what?

Sima: My lord, it's the army's job to fight wars. It's also their job to win them. Anything that could lead to defeat is strongly advised against.

King: But your plan doesn't look much like real fighting.

General: Ah, my lord, that's because your supreme highness needs to administer the coup de grâce when the time comes.

Chapter Five:

Where are you now?

Most people who love fighting, only know one way: Direct confrontation. Brute force pitted against brute force, but even a sumo wrestler knows that's not enough.

Sometimes called Positioning, this chapter is just a summary reminding the general that when two armies are evenly matched, the side that can think outside the battlefield will usually win, especially when it involves a clever surprise!

ACT FIVE

King: Who dares disturb his highness at this time of night?

Sima: My lord, we have come under attack. We must get to safety?

King: Under attack! By whom? Who would dare defile our lands with such aggression?

General: My lord, it appears our targeted neighbour discovered our plans to invade them. Quick my lord, we must hurry to safety.

Sima: Yes indeed, the hour is upon us, my lord. Time to rally the people and...

King: What about our plans - I fear they be ruined?

General: Nonsense my lord. We shall catch the enemy on the morrow like a flip of the palms. Our plans now have justifiable cause.

Chapter Six:

Where is the yin and yang of the battlefield?

Circumstances are forever changing. Forever in flux like rowing down whitewater rapids. Being able to flow with the downward currents to avoid the traps, that is the mark of a good navigator.

Sometimes just getting to the appointed field of battle is an adventure in itself. Let alone getting oneself in an advantageous position.

In other words, Suntzu advises that while you have strengths, try to find ways to turn your weaknesses into strengths as well.

ACT SIX

General: My lord, isn't this exciting?

King: General, how is running away from the enemy exciting - do tell?

General: Running away, my lord?

King: Yes. Running away.

General: My lord, I can assure his highness that we are doing no such thing. Our neighbour has decided to shoot first and ask questions later. Therefore, my lord, we react by doing a bit of Taichi.

King: Taichi?

Sima: Yes my lord. Taichi. Rather than resist their might, we step out of the way. And strike where they are weakest.

General: My lord, it would be better understood if one realises that the enemy attacked in haste, therefore they need a quick victory to overcome any deficiencies in planning.

Chapter Seven:

Can you dance the tango?

The Art of Manoeuvering is what separates a great general from a mediocre one. It's a good bet that the general you favour the most had this skill down pat!

And a general not skilled in this, is usually the one who ultimately loses.

But suppose both opposing generals are good at manoeuvering. What then?

Here Suntzu tries to highlight to the reader that there is more to maneuvering than just outflanking the enemy on the battlefield. While in some translations this chapter reads like a list of recommendations on what to look for in a good general, the recommendations can also be seen as a list ideas a general can use to outflank or outmaneuver the enemy.

The reason why Suntzu never seems to just come out and say things directly but always skirting around the bush with the Tao and stuff, is that there is a world of difference between talking frankly amongst peers and being delicate with those who have the ability to chop off one's head.

ACT SEVEN

King: All this marching is getting us nowhere! I feel like we have been going in circles. Is this not so?

Sima: Yes, my Lord, you are most correct.

King: What?

Sage: We are marching in a great big circle...

General: ...To avoid the enemy's brunt in exchange for some dinner.

Sima: What the general means my lord, is that we are going to attack their baggage train. Cut off their food supply and cut the fist off from the arm.

King: I don't fully comprehend this strategy. It doesn't seem very glorious to me.

General: War is rarely glorious, my lord.

Sima: My lord, what the General means to say is that the hour is upon us. We must make haste and attack their exposed vital point before their vanguard realises you are not where you are supposed to be and tries to regroup. By attacking their baggage train, the army gets a free feed at the enemy's expense. And you get free publicity back home as a winner.

General: Good news my lord, good news!

Chapter Eight:

Are we campaigning yet?

Usually called the Nine Variations or just Variations for short, the ninth chapter is about campaigning.

Here the assumption has been made that, at last, the order to proceed has been given. And things are finally moving forward.

As with all road trips, we may have a map, GSP and be well stocked up, including a tank full of petrol, but that does not mean we are ready for detours.

Hence, Suntzu lists a number of potential detours based on the shared experience and knowledge of countless generals like himself, and gives guidelines on what to do and not do should you come across any.

This includes the melodrama of internal politics which can sometimes be far more devastating to plans than a missing bridge.

ACT EIGHT

Sage: So there you have it, my lord. We have captured their supplies. And while their vanguard lays siege to one of our towns, we will sweep in behind them from the highground over there.

King: Brilliant. But won't they be expecting us to try and relieve the town?

General: Yes my lord. Normally you would be correct. But foreseeing that a situation like this might occur, we have bolstered the town's garrison in advance.

King: In advance?

Sage: Yes my lord

General: The town can hold out long enough for us to complete the enemy vanguard's encirclement.

King: And just for my understanding, why wouldn't the enemy just head straight for the capital?

Sage: The town is strategically located in such a way, that should it fall, it would appear that we have lost our will to fight.

King: Not possible!

General: Yes my lord. Possible.

King: Explain general! The will stands before you. Here. Now. I will not cower under my enemies because I lost a town.

Sima: My lord, the enemy has good reason to believe that you are in the town. In a manner of speaking.

General: My lord, the sun is setting in the west. And the enemy faces east upon the town. The troops are in position.

King: Very well. ...silently light the arrows. Archers! On my command!

Chapter Nine:

The army on the march

Sometimes things get lost in translation. And depending on which version of Suntzu's Art of War you have, the meaning of this chapter can either make sense or not.

Some versions call this chapter Mobilization. But the problem with that word, is that to most people it kind of implies how to get going. Yet in this chapter, the army is already on the march.

Here, what Suntzu requires us to understand is where and where not to fight.

And more importantly how to read the signs that a fight may be coming to you instead of the other way round. Not all things appear as they seem - whomever requires proof for their eyes to believe, they can be easily fooled.

ACT NINE

King: The vanguard has fallen! I accept their surrender.

General: My lord is most magnanimous. But we must stay on guard. Dawn is breaking and news is coming in indicating that a minority of the enemy's vanguard had escaped in last night's fiery mayhem.

Sima: My lord, I agree with the general. We must forego formalities in surrender.

King: Why? I am King. Is it not a king's right to see my enemy in chains before me?

Sima: It is a king's right. But a ceremony at this time could put us in a precarious position. We have only defeated their vanguard. General?

General: Might I suggest my lord, that we leave the defeated to be processed by the town garrison commander. And move the army over to here on the map?

Sima: That way, if the enemy's main army is on the march, we can force them away from here and be ready to counterstrike. And should they catch us, we will be on higher ground but we must make haste.

King: Gentlemen, your plan is sound. Break camp and march forth.

Chapter Ten:

Terrain - Going on the Offensive!

Whatever this chapter is usually called, this is the one most people glance over. And this is because it reads a bit like a repeat of the last chapter, chapter Nine.

On the surface, this is true. Suntzu talks about the different types of terrain (again) and what makes a good leader (again) in these situations.

But there is a difference.

Up 'til now, essentially a general would have been fighting a war on their home turf by home-turf rules.

This chapter is about going off field and fighting in someone else's field where the rules and conditions are different. In saying that, Suntzu stays delicately diplomatic because his bosses had egos a mile high: In their minds, if they have success in one area, then surely it was repeatable in another. Even if it meant imposing themselves on others.

So remember King Charles XII of Sweden, Emperor Napoleon I of France, and Hitler of Nazi Germany were all masters of their game on their turf i.e. Europe. Then each attacked Russia/the Soviet Union in their turn and the rules changed. It isn't necessarily that Russia is better at war than them, it's just that Russia is so scaled up vast, that it might as well be its own continent compared to almost all the countries of Europe combined.

So be smart: Recognise different games have different rules. And use the best players suited for each!

ACT TEN

King: You know what?

Sima: What my Lord?

King: I understand my father failed the first time. This is a massive country. Everything is so much vaster than ours. Their land sure makes fighting wars hard work.

Sima: It surely does my Lord.

General: And, my lord, much of our critical success will come from our ability to stay on the march. Avoiding the enemy's main force until our scouts can pinpoint where they actually are.

King: The terrain and weather here is not like back home.

Sima: Indeed my lord. We suspect that the enemy is using the home-advantage to wear us down. Already we have lost a few hundred soldiers because of the natural conditions imposed upon us.

General: So my lord, if we make camp here as indicated on our updated map, our men can rest in relative safety from the approaching storm over there.

Chapter Eleven:

What are the nine situations?

The nine classic situations, simply put, are the nine situations (there are always more, but nine is a good symbolic number) a leader could find themselves up shit creek.

These situations are nearly always not of one's choosing. So it is best to avoid them like the plague.

But should the path to victory mean you cannot avoid the obstacle, then it is best to eat a bit of humble pie and be aware of them beforehand by learning from the masters who have gone before and overcome them.

Overcome them and as Suntzu painstakingly advises: Turn the tables and use the nine situations against your opponent.

ACT ELEVEN

King: It seems, after these several weeks of marching around, that the enemy doesn't want to fight. Am I correct in this observation?

General: My lord, it is a tricky thing. Sometimes the cat is the mouse and the mouse is the cat. Which is which depends on who can out-dominate the chess board.

King: Perhaps we could force their hand - raise a few towns? That always works.

Sage: My lord, we have fought several battles now. And each time the enemy has bested us or outwitted us...

General: This may be our best option. Our spies indicate that we have found where their sovereign is encamped. By attacking this sizeable town over here. My lord.

King: The evidence points to that he will be forced to react. Sima, are we able to offset any surprise counterattacks from them?

Chapter Twelve:

The roof, the roof, the roof is on fire...

Chapter Twelve: Attack by fire. The nuclear option. The shortest chapter in Suntzu's book.

Every chapter he wrote, if you haven't noticed it before, is in fact actually two chapters combined as one. To every element there is a yang side and a yin side.

Each in its own way balances the other.

But sometimes there are things in this world, that by their very nature makes them inherently unstable. These things tend to usually only come with warning labels. Like fire.

That's one of the reasons this chapter is so short.

The first warning is to mind one's temperament.

The second warning is that fire is a weapon of last resort. And signals to all belligerents involved that playtime is over. The dummy has been spat.

Fire represents those deliberate acts that once done, you can never undo them or make things right again. Not even the justification of 'I didn't know... (blah, blah, blah)', will get you out of this one.

ACT TWELVE

Sima: My lord, it's done. As ordered, a small contingent is ransacking these villages over here. It will give the impression we are there.

King: Good. The chaos created will give space required to attack over here. Any indecision on their part will cost them dearly. General, are the trebuchets ready?

General: Yes my lord. Awaiting your command.

King: Very well. Bring it all down. Fire at will.

General: Trebuchets! On my mark! FIRE!

King: Sima, is our main army ready for our enemy?

Sima: Yes my lord. One quarter are engaged in attacking the town. The rest are on the high ground nearby waiting in ambush.

King: Good. It's going to be a long day.

General: All hail the King.

Chapter Thirteen:

Spies, lies and flies

The final frontier.

For those of you seeking gloriously mancho victory on the battlefield, you can stop here.

In fact, go back to chapter eleven and forget about ever having read chapter twelve, and certainly, verily, this chapter does not exist. Never has. Never will.

Complete blackout.

If you are, on the other hand, still here, is it possible that you're wondering why this chapter is last and not first?

The reason simple ...-ish.

While we live in a relatively peaceful world, most countries around the world are engaged in some sort of conflict with each other. It's a bit like sport really. There may be no comps running at the moment but teams still engage in friendlies.

And that's where spies and their lot come in. They usually operate as self-managed self-starters. They do what they do. Insider trading is a very high risk business best left to ghosts and shadows.

ACT THIRTEEN

Sima: WHAT!? ...What JUST happened?

General: We're under attack!

Sima: But how and where is his highness?

General: Men are searching the grounds as we speak. Banners have been spotted yonder.

Sima: We must find him quickly. Blast! This smoke...

General: Yes lieutenant... I see... Grim news indeed. Lieutenant... shore up our flank... Sima! The king has been found.

Sima: Where?

General: The enemy managed to penetrate our defences with assassins. He has been wounded. Sound the retreat.

Sima: Sound the retreat.

Chapter Fourteen:

There is no chapter fourteen

Modern convention dictates that I wrote a summary or conclusion as if The Introduction wasn't good enough.

After thirteen chapters Suntzu left it at that. His Art of War was complete and done.

He had found enlightenment through the military arts. And I am sure in China there are temples dedicated to him as a Celestial Worthy.

His Tao was The Art of War made writ.

And this concludes our meeting.

ACT FOURTEEN

The End

www.ingramcontent.com/pod-product-compliance
Lightning Source LLC
Chambersburg PA
CBHW071124240526
45465CB00023B/806